HARD NUTS OF HISTORY

Ultimate Quiz and Game Book

TRACEY TURNER

ILLUSTRATED BY JAMIE LENMAN

First published 2015 by

A & C Black, an imprint of Bloomsbury Publishing Plc

50 Bedford Square, London WC1B 3DP

www.bloomsbury.com

Bloomsbury is a registered trademark of Bloomsbury Publishing Plc

ISBN 978-1-4729-1096-7

A CIP catalogue for this book is available from the British Library.

Printed in China by Leo Paper Products, Heshan, Guangdong

1 3 5 7 9 10 8 6 4 2

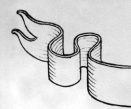

CONTENTS

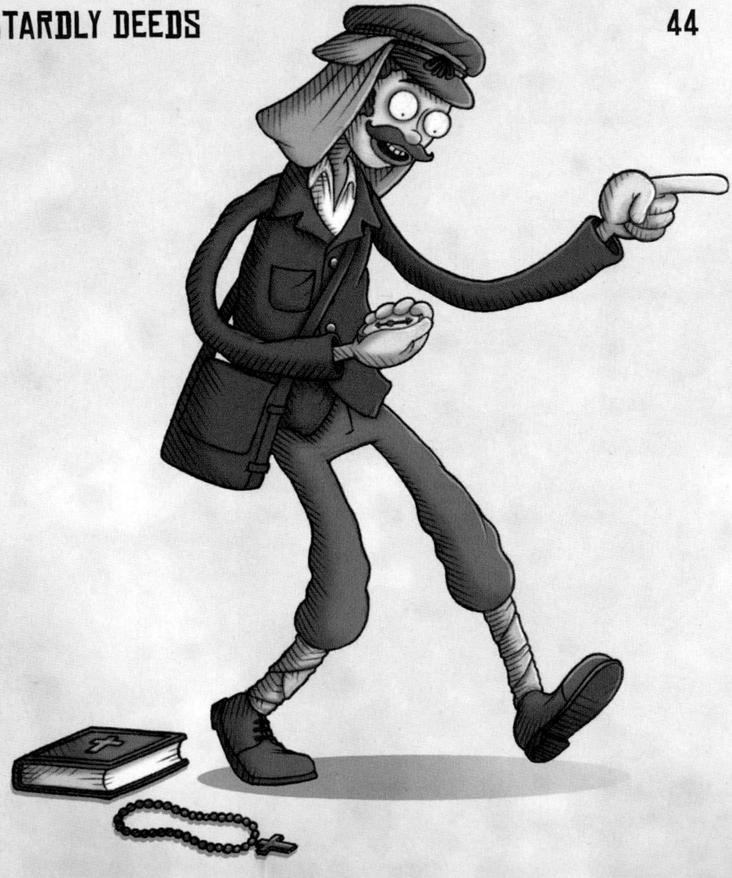

INTRODUCTION

How much do you know about some of the toughest men and women in history? This book is bursting with questions about warriors, conquerors, revolutionaries, pirates and more – some of them ruthless, some of them brave, and all of them as hard as nails.

DO YOU KNOW . . .

• How ten unlucky explorers met their untimely ends?

• What to do with a nest of bees?

• Which heads belong to which Egyptian gods?

• Which English hero died at the Battle of Trafalgar?

Plus, play a mummy-making game to see if you can prepare a dead body for the afterlife, and roll a dice to find out if you and your army of cut-throat soldiers can conquer a vast empire.

If you've ever wanted to set sail on the high seas for a life of crime, meet a falcon-headed god, or battle the Hittites, read on . . .

Plus turn to page 63 and create your own royal or pirate name!

WARNING: THIS QUIZ BOOK IS NOT FOR THE FAINT-HEARTED!

NAME THAT VIKING!

The Vikings were fond of nicknames, but they weren't always complimentary. Choose from the multiple choices below and see if you can match these Vikings to their nicknames.

1. Founder of the first settlement on Greenland, Eric the . . .

a) Black

b) Grey

c) Green

d) Red

2. Legendary Norse ruler, Ragnar . . .

a) Furry Face

b) Hairy Breeches

c) Hairy Head

d) Bushy Moustache

3. Ragnar's son and Viking king, Sigurd . . .

a) Snake-in-the-eye

b) Snake-in-the-grass

c) Snake Hips

d) Snake Charmer

RAGNAR . . .

4. King of Denmark and Norway, Harald . . .

a) Red Nose

b) Brown Eyes

c) Blue Tooth

d) White Beard

5. Viking warrior (and another of Ragnar's sons), Ivar the . . .

a) Skinless

b) Boneless

c) Gutless

d) Legless

IVAR THE . . .

6. Viking explorer who sailed to North America, Leif the . . .

a) Unlucky

b) Lucky

c) Happy

d) Sad

7. Norwegian king, Ketill . . .

a) Flatnose

b) Longnose

c) Littlenose

d) Runnynose

8. King of Sweden, and brother of Sigurd and Ivar, Bjorn . . .

a) Goldbeard

b) Ironside

c) Silverside

d) Steelgrip

9. King of Norway and Northumbria, Eric . . .

a) Bloodaxe

b) Bloodspear

c) Bloodsword

d) Bloodbow

10. The first king of Norway, Harald . . .

a) Baldy

b) Beardy

c) Finehair

d) Curlyhair

ERIC . . .

11. Kublai Khan was suspicious of foreign visitors and refused to meet any.

12. Attila the Hun led his Huns against Genghis Khan.

13. Ordono the Wicked was King of Spain in the 900s and succeeded Sancho the Fat.

14. King Ashurnasipal of Assyria claimed to have personally killed 450 lions.

15. Julius Caesar was kidnapped by pirates.

ATTILA THE HUN

16. Xerxes the Great of Persia whipped the sea with chains after a storm destroyed a bridge.

17. Ivan the Terrible killed his own son.

18. Roman Emperor Caligula ordered his soldiers to collect seashells.

19. Shi Huangdi, the first emperor of China, had scholars buried alive for owning forbidden books.

20. Pisistratus became the first tyrant of Athens in ancient Greece when he rode into the city on a war elephant.

IVAN THE TERRIBLE

PISISTRATUS

ANSWERS

1. True

2. False
She battered the Romans at Colchester before she was defeated.

3. False
He was Tarquin the Proud, who ruled until he was turfed off the throne in 509 BC, when the Roman Republic began.

4. True
Mary Queen of Scots was the daughter of James V of Scotland, Elizabeth's first cousin – so Mary Queen of Scots and Elizabeth I were first cousins once removed.

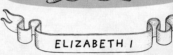

ELIZABETH I

5. True

6. True

7. False
Hatshepsut was the first female pharaoh. She ruled around 1470 BC.

8. True

9. False
He was imprisoned by the Spanish and died during a riot.

10. True
He also named lots of cities after himself.

HATSHEPSUT

11. False
Marco Polo, from Venice, lived in China and became a favourite of the Mongol emperor Kublai Khan's.

12. False
Genghis Khan was born 700 years after Attila the Hun.

13. True

14. True
He immortalised his daring deeds in inscriptions in his palace.

15. True
He got his revenge by having them executed.

16. True

17. True

18. True
He did lots of strange things, including dressing as a god and drinking pearls dissolved in vinegar.

19. True

20. False
He tricked everyone into thinking he'd been attacked, and they voted in favour of him having an armed bodyguard – which he used to overthrow the city.

GENGHIS KHAN

CONQUERING GAME

For two to six players. You'll need a counter each and a dice to play this game.

You have a large army of desperate cut-throat soldiers at your disposal and you're in the mood for some conquering. Have you got what it takes to conquer a vast empire?

LEGENDARY HARD NUT HEROES QUIZ

In myths and legends, hard nuts can be even tougher than real life ones, and much more alarming. Choose from the multiple choices below and find out how much you know about some of history's toughest legendary heroes.

1. Roman hero Aeneas founded a city where he saw which of the following?

a) A pig and its piglets

b) An eagle swooping on a hare

c) A wolf guarding its cubs

2. From which of these did legendary Irish hero Finn McCool gain his extraordinary knowledge?

a) The Tree of Knowledge

b) A magic owl

c) The Salmon of Knowledge

3. Greek hero Jason was helped by the sorceress Medea in his quest for . . .

a) Three golden apples

b) A flying horse

c) A golden fleece

FINN MCCOOL

4. Which English hero robbed from the rich to give to the poor?

a) John O'Groats

b) Robin Hood

c) Dick Whittington

5. Sir Gawain, Knight of King Arthur's Round Table, fought a . . .

a) White Serpent

b) Green Knight

c) Red Dragon

6. Which Greek hero had to complete 12 tasks including killing the nine-headed hydra, and fetching a three headed dog from the underworld?

a) Perseus

b) Medea

c) Heracles

7. Native American Indians tell stories about an animal hero, Clever . . .

a) Buffalo

b) Mountain Lion

c) Coyote

SIR GAWAIN

8. East African hero Fumo Liyongo could only be killed by . . .

a) A silver arrow

b) A copper dagger

c) A bronze sword

9. Greek hero Theseus killed which of the following?

a) The Gorgon, Medusa

b) The Minotaur

c) The Sphinx

10. Beowulf, the super-strong Swedish hero, killed . . .

a) Grendel, a man-eating monster

b) Gretchen, a man-eating tiger

c) Grenville, a man-eating bull

BEOWULF

Answers: 1a), 2c), 3c), 4b), 5b), 6c), 7c), 8b), 9b), 10a).

GRUESOME ENDS QUIZ

Hard nuts often meet with terrible ends. Do you know what fate had in store for this band of toughies? Chose from the multiple choices below and find out what sticky ends were in store for some of history's hardest nuts.

WARNING: THIS QUIZ IS NOT FOR THE FAINT-HEARTED. IT'S PRETTY GRUESOME!

1. Attila the Hun didn't suffer the kind of violent death you might imagine – he died from which of the following?

a) A nosebleed

b) A sprained ankle

c) A cold

2. The pirate Blackbeard was killed by the English Navy and had his head chopped off. According to legend, what happened next?

a) His body swam around his ship

b) His disembodied head cursed the English navy

c) His body picked up a sword and killed three English officers

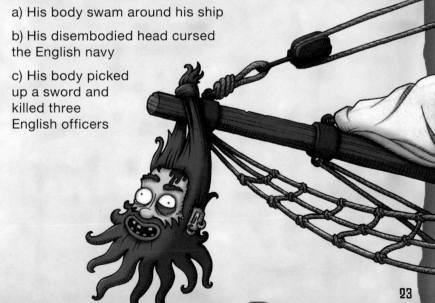

3. Warrior queen Boudica refused to be captured by the Romans, who had defeated her army, so she . . .

a) Went into hiding for the rest of her life

b) Poisoned herself

c) Drowned herself in the sea

4. What happened to French heroine Joan of Arc when she was captured by the English?

a) She was beheaded

b) She was burnt at the stake

c) She was hanged

JOAN OF ARC

5. How did William the Conqueror die?

a) He was stabbed by a treacherous soldier

b) His horse stumbled and he injured himself on the saddle

c) He tripped over a kneeling peasant and impaled himself on a spike

6. Julius Caesar was stabbed to death – who stabbed him?

a) 23 politicians

b) His own bodyguard

c) His own wife

JULIUS CAESAR

7. What killed US president Abraham Lincoln?

a) He accidentally swallowed poison

b) He fell off a balcony

c) He was shot by an assassin

8. Egyptian pharaoh Cleopatra killed herself by . . .

a) Letting a venomous snake bite her

b) Jumping into the crocodile-infested River Nile

c) Letting a deadly scorpion sting her

9. What happened to Vercingetorix the Gaul, deadly enemy of Julius Caesar?

a) He became friends with Julius Caesar and died fighting in battle alongside him

b) Julius Caesar had him executed

c) He leapt from the tallest tower of his castle rather than surrender to Caesar

10. Agrippina the Younger, mother of Roman Emperor Nero, was assassinated by Nero after several murder attempts including . . .

a) Venomous spiders let loose in her bedroom

b) Sinking the boat she was travelling in

c) A booby-trapped collapsing bed

EMPEROR NERO

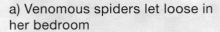

Answers: 1a), 2a), 3b), 4b), 5b), 6a), 7c), 8a), 9b), 10c).

25

HEADLESS GODS

The ancient Egyptians had lots of different gods, with a wide variety of interesting and alarming animal heads. Can you match the right head to their Egyptian god name?

1. Horus, god of the sky.

2. Anubis, god of the dead.

3. Bastet, goddess of protection.

4. Heryshef, creator god and god of the riverbanks.

5. Thoth, god of knowledge, wisdom and hieroglyphs.

6. Heket, goddess of childbirth.

7. Sobek, god of the River Nile.

8. Sekhmet, goddess of war.

9. Geb, god of the earth.

10. Satet, goddess of hunting and the Nile flood.

Answers: 1) Falcon, 2) Jackal, 3) Cat, 4) Ram, 5) Ibis (but is also sometimes represented as a baboon), 6) Frog, 7) Crocodile, 8) Lioness, 9) Goose, 10) Woman with antelope horns.

BATTLES QUIZ

History is full of countless battles. But how much do you really know about them? Chose from the multiple choices below and find out how well you know your battle history.

1. At which battle did Custer make his last stand?

a) The Alamo

b) Shiloh

c) Little Bighorn

d) Fort Sumter

2. The Battle of the Somme was an especially bloody battle during which of these wars?

a) The First World War

b) The Second World War

c) The American Revolutionary War

d) The Vietnam War

3. Which English hero died at the Battle of Trafalgar?

a) Alfred the Great

b) Lord Nelson

c) The Duke of Wellington

d) Sir Walter Raleigh

GENERAL CUSTER

LORD NELSON

4. The Battle of Agincourt in 1415 was part of which war?

a) The Hundred Years' War

b) The Seven Years' War

c) The Six Months' War

d) The Ten-minute War

5. Which of these battles was the last one fought by Napoleon Bonaparte?

a) The Battle of Tours

b) The Battle of Waterloo

c) The Battle of the Nile

d) The Battle of Trafalgar

6. Where was the Battle of the Alamo fought?

a) Mississippi

b) Maryland

c) Tennessee

d) Texas

7. Which of these famous Scots fought at the Battle of Culloden?

a) Bonnie Prince Charlie

b) Robert the Bruce

c) William Wallace

d) Rob Roy

NAPOLEON BONAPARTE

8. Which of these battles was fought between Britain and Germany's air forces in the Second World War?

a) The Battle of the Skies

b) The Battle of Germany

c) The Battle of Britain

d) The Battle of the Aeroplanes

9. The poem *The Charge of the Light Brigade* by Rudyard Kipling is about which of these battles?

a) The Battle of Balaclava during the Crimean War

b) The Battle of Britain during the Second World War

c) The Battle of Isandlwana during the Zulu War

d) The Battle of Edgehill during the English Civil War

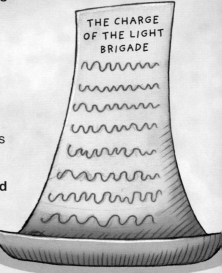

THE CHARGE OF THE LIGHT BRIGADE

10. The Battle of Naseby was fought in the English Civil War between the Cavaliers and . . . ?

a) The Longheads

b) The Squareheads

c) The Roundheads

d) The Coneheads

11. Which of these battles did American hero Davy Crockett fight in?

a) The Battle of Gettysburg

b) The Battle of Yorktown

c) The Battle of Charleston

d) The Battle of the Alamo

DAVY CROCKETT

12. The Battle of Bosworth Field was the last major battle in . . . ?

a) The War of the Roses

b) The War of Jenkins' Ear

c) The Peninsula War

d) The Peasants' Revolt

13. Which of these kings fought in the Battle of the Boyne?

a) William the Conqueror

b) William of Orange

c) Edward the Confessor

d) Charles I

14. The Battle of Qadesh was fought using . . .

a) Tanks and machine guns

b) War elephants

c) Horse-drawn war chariots

d) Crossbows

15. The Battle of Iwo Jima was fought during which of these wars?

a) The Vietnam War

b) The First World War

c) The Second World War

d) The Russian Civil War

Answers: 1c), 2a), 3b), 4a), 5b), 6d), 7a), 8c), 9a), 10c), 11d), 12a) By the way, there really was a War of Jenkins' Ear, 13b), 14c), 15c).

31

EXPLORERS AND THEIR UNTIMELY ENDS

Hard nut explorers set out on intrepid adventures into icy wastes, sweltering deserts and dense jungles. Many of them met with deadly danger, and some of them never returned. Can you match these explorers to their terrible fates? Turn to the answers on page 34 to see if you're right.

1 Amelia Earhart

2 Captain Scott

3 John Speke

4 Captain Cook

5 Ferdinand Magellan

6 Mungo Park

7 Walter Raleigh

8 Ponce de Leon

9 Burke and Wills

10 Alexandrine Tinné

a) Shot himself while hunting

b) Died from sickness, starvation and exposure in the Australian outback

c) Disappeared in the Pacific Ocean

d) Killed by Philippine islanders

e) Died from an arrow wound in the New World

f) Murdered in the Sahara Desert

g) Disappeared in Africa

h) Froze to death in Antarctica

i) Beheaded by King James I

j) Hacked to death by Hawaiian islanders

ANSWERS

1 c) Earhart was attempting to fly her plane around the world.

2 h) Captain Scott and some of his team froze to death just over ten miles short of supplies that could have helped them.

3 a) No one knows whether it was an accident or if Speke did it on purpose.

4 j) Cook's body was cut up and divided amongst the Hawaiian chiefs, but bits were returned to his ship for burial.

5 d) Magellan's team carried on without him and successfully circumnavigated the world.

6 g) No one knows exactly what happened to Park.

7 i) King James had Raleigh imprisoned for years, then let him out for a bit of exploring – but it didn't go as well as he'd hoped (plus he'd never liked him anyway), so he had Raleigh executed.

8 e) Ponce de Leon was the first European to land in Florida, where he was wounded by a Native American arrow.

9 b) Burke and Wills were the first Europeans to cross Australia from south to north.

10 f) It's thought that Tinné's murderers believed she was carrying a fortune in gold.

ODD HARD NUT OUT

All of the following people are hard nuts, but in each group of four there's an odd one out. Can you spot them?

1. Three of these ancient Greeks are generals, one is a philosopher.

a) Alcibiades

b) Pericles

c) Socrates

d) Themistocles

2. Three of these women from the ancient world are warrior queens, one is a scholar.

a) Zenobia

b) Artemisia

c) Hypatia

d) Tomyris

3. Three of these hard nuts are enemies of ancient Rome, one is an ancient Roman.

a) Hannibal

b) Vercingetorix

c) Boudica

d) Sulla

4. Three of these are heroes from mythology, one is a monster.

a) Achilles

b) Cú Chullain

c) Gilgamesh

d) Huwawa

5. Three of these women are pirates, one is an explorer.

a) Mary Kingsley

b) Anne Bonny

c) Grace O'Malley

d) Mary Read

6. Three of these ancient Egyptian pharaohs are men, one is a woman.

a) Tutankhamun

b) Hatshepsut

c) Seqenenre

d) Thutmose

7. Three of these ancient Romans are generals, one is a doctor.

a) Pompey

b) Galen

c) Scipio

d) Mark Antony

8. Three of these intrepid explorers went to the New World, one went to Africa.

a) Walter Raleigh

b) Christopher Columbus

c) David Livingstone

d) Ponce de Leon

9. Three of these are generals, one is a general's horse.

a) Bucephalus

b) Pelopidas

c) Scipio

d) Themistocles

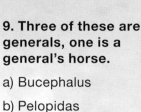

10. Three of these Native American warriors are from the Sioux tribe, one is an Apache.

a) Crazy Horse

b) Geronimo

c) Sitting Bull

d) Red Cloud

MUMMY MAKING GAME

For two to six players. You'll need a counter each and a dice to play this game.

START THE MUMMIFICATION PROCESS HERE.

2

Successfully extract brain through nose. Go forward three squares.

Drop bottle of expensive resins. Go back three squares.

Wet weather interferes with the drying process. Go back four squares.

13

Treat the dried body with oils and resins. Go forward three squares.

Complete mummification of the dead person's pet cat. Go forward three squares.

23 22 21

Miss a go while you buy lucky charms for the mummy.

Place your complete mummy inside a coffin with the Book of the Dead. Go forward two squares.

26

Making an Egyptian mummy in the correct way is important – get it wrong and your mummy will miss out on eternal life. Can you ensure that this person makes it to the afterlife?

ABSOLUTELY ANCIENT QUIZ

Not only is this quiz absolutely ancient, it's absolutely enormous as well. But is it absolutely impossible? Only you can answer that. Chose from the multiple choices below and find out if you can answer absolutely every question right!

1. Which ancient Roman leader was stabbed to death by 23 politicians?

a) Augustus Caesar

b) Julius Caesar

c) Caligula

d) Nero

2. What did dead ancient Egyptians need to help them get to the afterlife?

a) The Water of the Dead

b) The Food of the Dead

c) The Book of the Dead

d) The Crown of the Dead

3. Shihuangdi united which country in 206 BC?

a) Greece

b) Assyria

c) India

d) China

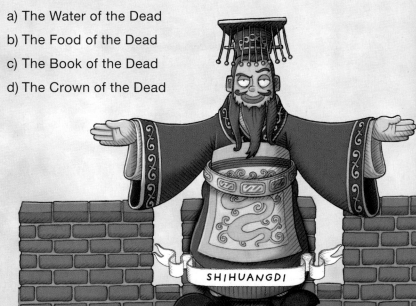

SHIHUANGDI

4. Which of these were enemies of ancient Egypt?

a) The Celts

b) The Carthaginians

c) The Huns

d) The Hittites

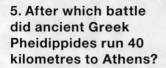

5. After which battle did ancient Greek Pheidippides run 40 kilometres to Athens?

a) Battle of Salamis

b) Battle of Thermopylae

c) Battle of Marathon

d) Battle of Nike

6. Which country did the Qin dynasty rule in the 200s BC?

a) Persia

b) China

c) India

d) Japan

7. Who united Egypt around 5,000 years ago?

a) Tutankhamun

b) Narmer

c) Thutmose

d) Cleopatra

8. Who marched elephants over the Alps Mountains in 218 BC?

a) Alexander the Great

b) Hannibal

c) Julius Caesar

d) Pompey the Great

9. Which Persian king was defeated by Alexander the Great?

a) Cyrus the Great

b) Xerxes the Great

c) Darius III

d) Cyrus the Cowardly

ALEXANDER THE GREAT

10. Which of these were NOT enemies of ancient Rome?

a) The Huns

b) The Visigoths

c) The Celts

d) The Hyksos

11. Which enemy of Rome was beaten at the Battle of Watling Street?

a) Cleopatra

b) Caractacus

c) Boudica

d) Vercingetorix

THE . . .

12. Which country was conquered by King Cambyses of Persia in 525 BC?

a) Assyria

b) Egypt

c) Greece

d) Arabia

13. Who did Rome fight in the Punic Wars?

a) Carthage

b) Britain

c) Gaul

d) Greece

14. Which sea battle was fought between ancient Romans Octavian and Mark Antony?

a) The Battle of Actium

b) The Battle of Salamis

c) The Battle of Trafalgar

d) The Battle of Jutland

15. Which ancient city had famous Hanging Gardens?

a) Rome

b) Athens

c) Memphis

d) Babylon

16. Who worshipped gods including Zeus, Poseidon and Hermes?

a) The ancient Romans

b) The ancient Greeks

c) The Carthaginians

d) The ancient Egyptians

17. What is Draco, an ancient Greek, famous for?

a) Making harsh laws

b) Winning a sea battle against the Persians

c) Writing plays

d) Sticking his enemies' heads on spikes

18. Ashurbanipal was a king of . . .

a) Assyria

b) India

c) Persia

d) Athens

19. The modern city of Luxor is built partly on the site of which ancient city?

a) Alexandria

b) Rome

c) Halicarnassus

d) Thebes

DRACO

20. Which empire destroyed Babylon in 1595 BC?

a) The Hittite Empire

b) The Persian Empire

c) The Mongol Empire

d) The Ottoman Empire

Answers: 1b), 2c) The Book of the Dead was put inside the mummy's coffin, 3d), 4d), 5c), 6b), 7b), 8b), 9c) There wasn't really a Cyrus the Cowardly, 10d) The Hyksos once ruled ancient Egypt, but they were long gone by the time of the Romans, 11c) 12b), 13a), 14a), 15d), 16b), 17a), 18a), 19d), 20a), 'draconian' to describe a harsh law from Draco.

DASTARDLY DEEDS

These hard nuts could become very violent when roused. But which of these terrible deeds are true? Choose from the multiple choices below and see how well you know your dastardly deeds. In each case, two of the options are made up.

WARNING: THIS QUIZ IS NOT FOR THE FAINT-HEARTED. IT'S PRETTY GRUESOME!

1. Queen Tomyris of the Massagetae in Central Asia . . .

a) Used her enemy's skin to cover a book

b) Used her enemy's scalp as a hair ornament

c) Used her enemy's skull as a drinking cup

2. Grace O'Malley, the Irish pirate . . .

a) Showered her enemies with flaming arrows

b) Poured molten lead on her enemies' heads

c) Poured buckets of cow manure on her enemies' heads

3. Genghis Khan, leader of the Mongol tribes . . .

a) Punished an entire tribe by branding everyone with the word 'traitor'

b) Punished an entire tribe by killing everyone over certain height

c) Punished an entire tribe by chopping off everyone's thumbs

GRACE O'MALLEY

4. Spartacus, leader of the Roman slave rebellion . . .

a) Made a daring escape armed with kitchen utensils

b) Stole the weapons of an entire Roman legion to make a daring escape

c) Made a daring escape armed with garden tools

5. Scottish rebel leader William Wallace . . .

a) Roasted his dead English enemy on a spit

b) Had an English enemy's dead body skinned and made into a belt

c) Tied his dead English enemy to a tree and pelted him with rotten fruit

6. Ivan the Terrible, Tsar of Russia . . .

a) Ordered his private army to destroy a city and kill thousands of its innocent citizens

b) Ordered his private army to kill the prime minister and the rest of the Russian government

c) Ordered his private army to run away

WILLIAM WALLACE

7. Attila, leader of the feared barbarian tribe the Huns, demanded gold from the Byzantine Empire in return for not invading and then. . .

a) Used the gold to buy a palace overlooking the Byzantine capital

b) Ran away with the emperor's wife

c) Invaded anyway

8. Aurangzeb, conquering Mughal Emperor . . .

a) Imprisoned his sons and daughters

b) Killed three of his brothers and imprisoned his father

c) Imprisoned his 97 wives

ATTILA THE HUN

9. King Aella of Northumbria threw his Viking enemy into . . .

a) A lake full of crocodiles

b) A cave full of vampire bats

c) A pit full of venomous snakes

10. Wu Zeitan, Empress of China . . .

a) Had her daughter-in-law starved to death

b) Had her daughter and son-in-law burnt at the stake

c) Had her son-in-law tickled to death

AURANGZEB

Answers: 1c), 2b), 3b), 4a), 5b), 6a), 7c), 8b), 9c), 10a).

46

GREEK MONSTERS AND HEROES QUIZ

Greek myths are full of monstrous creatures, horrible deaths, and super-strong, brave heroes. How much do you know about them? Choose from the multiple choices below and test your monster knowledge!

1. Medusa the gorgon could turn victims to stone just by looking at them. She was . . .

a) A giant spider with eight mesmerising eyes

b) Part snake, part eagle, part lion

c) A woman with snakes for hair

2. Perseus killed Medusa and rescued beautiful Andromeda from a . . .

a) Sea monster

b) Giant

c) Monstrous bull

3. The Minotaur, part man and part bull, lived in a . . .

a) Palace in Athens

b) Swamp on the island of Kos

c) Labyrinth on the island of Crete

4. The Echidna, mother to various monsters including the Hydra, Cerberus and the Sphinx, was . . .

a) Part snake, part woman

b) A one-eyed giant fish

c) A flying rat

5. Which hero tamed and rode the flying horse, Pegasus?

a) Perseus

b) Odysseus

c) Bellerophon

6. What guarded the Underworld?

a) A nine-headed dragon

b) A three-headed dog

c) A hundred-headed swamp monster

7. Which Greek hero had a vulnerable heel?

a) Agamemnon

b) Achilles

c) Actaeon

8. The sphinx stopped travellers on their way to Thebes. If they couldn't answer her riddle she . . .

a) Ate them up

b) Tied them to a stake and sang to them

c) Threw them off a cliff to a man-eating octopus

9. The hero Odysseus sailed to the island of Circe the witch. She turned his crew into . . .

a) Sheep

b) Cows

c) Pigs

10. The Graeae were the Gorgons' sisters. They shared . . .

a) A husband

b) A brain

c) An eye and a tooth

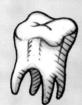

GREEK MONSTERS AND LADDERS GAME

Play this game as you would snakes and ladders, using a counter for each player and a dice.

If you arrive at a monster's head, you have to slide down to the tip of its tail. If you land at the bottom of a ladder, climb up to the top of it. Challenge your friends and family and see who can make it to the end first!

WHICH RAMPAGING CONQUEROR AM I?

History is bursting full of ruthless rampaging conquerors – can you figure out who said each of the statements below? Try matching the statements to the portraits of the conquerors.

1. I was born in a Mongolia tribe and conquered the second-largest empire there's ever been.

XERXES THE GREAT

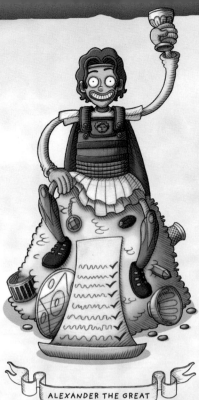

2. I became King of Macedonia when I was 20, and spent the next 12 years conquering as far away as India.

ALEXANDER THE GREAT

3. As Duke of Normandy I invaded Britain, defeated the English king and took his crown.

GENGHIS KHAN

4. I ruled the Persian Empire and wanted to make Greece part of it, but failed.

ATTILA THE HUN

5. I was king of a barbarian tribe at the end of the Roman Empire.

WILLIAM THE CONQUEROR

Answers: 1 Genghis Khan, 2 Alexander the Great, 3 William the Conqueror, 4 Xerxes the Great, 5 Attila the Hun

WILD WOMEN QUIZ

History is littered with hard nut women, but they aren't always as famous as male hard nuts. Chose from the multiple choices below and find out how much you know about these wild women.

1. The Trung sisters are heroines from which country?

a) Hawaii

b) Vietnam

c) Russia

2. Zenobia, Queen of Palmyra in Syria, conquered an empire but was defeated by . . .

a) The Hittites

b) The Romans

c) The Persians

3. Which French leader died in 1431 and was made a saint?

a) Bernadette of Lourdes

b) Joan of Arc

c) Genevieve of Paris

ZENOBIA

4. Which Celtic queen ruled the Iceni tribe?

a) Cartimandua

b) Columba

c) Boudica

5. Female warrior Tomoe Gozen was which of the following?

a) A crusading knight

b) A Japanese samurai

c) A Viking warrior

6. Which queen defeated Cyrus the Great?

a) Tomyris

b) Elizabeth I

c) Cleopatra

7. Agrippina was the wife of Emperor Claudius (and probably his murderer) and the mother of which other Roman emperor?

a) Augustus

b) Hadrian

c) Nero

8. Violette Szabo and Noor Inayat Khan were both . . . ?

a) Special agents in the Second World War

b) Female soldiers in the Russian Civil War

c) Nurses in the Crimean War

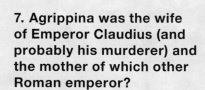

TOMOE GOZEN

9. Which Victorian woman explored the Ogooue River by canoe, met a crocodile, climbed Mount Cameroon, and became an expert on African insects?

a) Florence Nightingale

b) Mary Ann Evans

c) Mary Kingsley

10. What is hard nut Harriet Tubman famous for?

a) Running an escape route for slaves in America

b) Running an escape route for Jews out of Nazi Germany

c) Running an escape route for slaves in ancient Rome

HARRIET TUBMAN

PIRATE GAME

For two to six players. You'll need a counter each and a dice to play this game.

BEGIN YOUR PIRATE ADVENTURE HERE. ARRRR.

2

3

Ship runs aground on sand bar. Go back three squares.

11

Outbreak of scurvy aboard ship. Go back two squares to stock up on citrus fruit.

Board merchant vessel and capture loot! Go forward three squares.

Sighted by naval vessel. Run away to square six.

14

The navy catch up with your pirate ship. Go back three squares.

Miss a go while you bury your treasure.

22

Avast there! You've taken to the high seas for a life of crime as a ruthless pirate in the Caribbean. Will you live long enough to spend your retirement gloating over your ill-gotten gains?

Flogged for brawling. Go back two squares.

6

Spot a likely ship to raid. Go forward three squares.

Marooned on a desert island for inciting mutiny. Miss two goes.

8

Injured in fight aboard merchant ship. Miss a go while you recover.

16

17

Shipwrecked on reef! Go back five squares.

19

Walk the plank in shark infested waters. Go back to the start.

24

Return to the island, recover treasure, and live a life of luxury for the rest of your days!

MATCH THE DEADLY ENEMIES

Hard nuts wouldn't be hard nuts unless they had some deadly enemies to contend with. Can you match each hard nut below with their deadly enemy? Turn to the answers on page 62 to see how well you did.

1. Tomyris (Queen of the Massagetae tribe)

2. Spartacus (Roman slave rebel)

3. Vercingetorix (Gaulish king)

4. Boudica (Celtic British Queen)

5. Napoleon (French revolutionary general)

6. William Wallace (Scottish rebel)

7. Harold I of England

8. Ulysses S Grant (American general)

9. Cleopatra (Egyptian queen)

10. Sitting Bull (Native American Indian chief)

a) Crassus (Roman general)

b) King Edward I of England

c) Lieutenant Colonel Custer (American general)

d) Cyrus the Great (Persian emperor)

e) Wellington (British general)

f) William the Conqueror

g) Robert E Lee (American general)

h) Octavian (Roman general)

i) Suetonius Paulinus (Roman governor of Britain)

j) Julius Caesar (Roman general)

ANSWERS

1 d) Cyrus was trying to add Tomyris' kingdom to his empire, but she defeated him and it's said she cut off his head and used his skull as a drinking cup.

2 a) Spartacus' slave rebellion was finally done for when Crassus led the Roman army against him.

3 j) Vercingetorix stood up to Julius Caesar, who was conquering Gaul, but he was defeated in the end and executed by Caesar.

4 i) Boudica was defeated in battle by Suetonius Paulinus, but not before she'd done some serious damage.

5 e) Napoleon was defeated by Wellington at the Battle of Waterloo.

6 b) Edward I is also known as 'the Hammer of the Scots' was William Wallace's deadly enemy.

7 f) Harold died at the Battle of Hastings, while William the Conqueror became the new king of England.

8 g) Grant and Lee were on opposite sides in the American Civil War.

9 h) Octavian defeated Cleopatra and her boyfriend, Mark Antony, and went on to become Augustus, the first emperor of Rome.

10 c) Sitting Bull fought Custer at the Battle of the Little Big Horn and won.

EDWARD I

THE NAME GENERATOR

Have you ever wanted to be a pirate, or a member of royalty? Make a start by giving yourself the right sort of name. Pick one word from each of the three columns (or you could use your own first name instead of the middle column) and simple as that, you've got your own pirate or royal name. Don't forget to accessorise with parrots, eye patches, crowns or sceptres.

PIRATE NAME GENERATOR

Captain	Bart/Meg	Silver/Gold
First Mate	Jack/Kate	Diamond/Pearl/Ruby
Cabin Boy/Girl	Sam/Liz	Inkheart
Privateer	Bill/Annie	Crossbones
Peg-leg	Pete/Mary	Cutlass
Crazy	Ben/Kitty	Flintlock

ROYAL NAME GENERATOR

King or Queen	Frederick/Elizabeth	the Great
Sultan	Ivan/Katerina	the Wise
Emperor or Empress	Mehmet/Talia	the Beautiful
Tsar or Tsarina	Osman/Anastasia	the Magnificent
Prince or Princess	Henry/Mary	the Conqueror
Duke or Duchess	Claudius/Julia	the All Powerful